create and display

Inspiring Learning Environments

Full of exciting activities and displays for the whole curriculum

Ages 4–11
for all primary years

Nathalie Frost

Book End, Range Road, Witney, Oxfordshire, OX29 OYD
www.scholastic.co.uk
© 2011, Scholastic Ltd
1 2 3 4 5 6 7 8 9   0 1 2 3 4 5 6 7 8 9

British Library Cataloguing-in-Publication Data
A catalogue record for this book is available from the
British Library.

ISBN 978-1407-12526-8
Printed by Bell & Bain Ltd, Glasgow

Text © Nathalie Frost 2011

Commissioning Editor
Paul Naish

Development Editor
Emily Jefferson

Editors
Fliss Bage and Simon Bage

Series Designer and Cover Design
Andrea Lewis and Sarah Garbett

Designer
Tracey Camden

Photography
Steve Forrest and Gareth Boden

Acknowledgements

The author and publisher would like to thank the
children and staff of The Rosary School, Holy Trinity
C of E, and Holy Trinity and St Silas, London for
all their support and hard work, and the beautiful
artwork featured in the displays in this book.

Nathalie Frost would like to say a special thank
you to Richard Reinhardt and Love Art for
Schools, their growing and inspiring company
(www.loveartforschools.com).

Lastly, the author would like to thank her
grandmother, Margaret Charles, for sharing with
her and teaching her to look at the beauty that is all
around us.

Contents

Introduction

Creating an inspiring learning environment is an essential part of running a successful classroom. This is the space in which not only you as an educator but every child in the class will spend most of their time every day. It is so important to make it as informative and as exciting as you can. Most of us at some point have experienced a run-down old space with pictures, posters and information that have clearly been there for months if not years. It is totally uninspiring. In contrast, think of a room, a workspace, a shop or a waiting room you've visited that has made you interested, lifted you and left you feeling like you'd be happy to visit the space again. Behind such a space someone is taking responsibility and hoping that the visitor will be left interested and perhaps even inspired.

Children are constantly stimulated by changing images in their immediate environment. The television, the internet, advertisement billboards, computer games, and eye-catching and often intriguing visual imagery are all around. The world is so full of colour, both in the manufactured and the natural world. What we take in and process is, of course, another thing.

We need to ensure that what the children experience visually within the classroom is actually *seen* by them and not ignored; getting them involved is a key way of keeping them interested. Share with them your plans for the classroom if possible; older children may wish to help decide which space is most appropriate for certain displays.

Classrooms need to be comfortable, warm environments. While using plenty of colours to cheer up a space, we also need to make sure it is not too distracting. For example, bright backing paper can be great occasionally if displaying monotone pieces of work, such as writing and pencil drawings, but if the children's work is already very colourful it should be the main focal point, so consider toning down the background so that you can focus on what is important.

The classroom is a place for interesting images and artefacts. Making small pictures or creating individual models is as important as a huge whole-wall or communal display. Each activity can be displayed and presented and can go towards creating your own unique inspiring learning environment. Take children on visits to a variety of different environments. As well as museums and galleries, if possible walk to parks or open spaces, allowing them to discover how important an environment is, and to understand the effects it can have on how we feel and respond and learn.

Small areas of the room can be transformed using the children's work. Try to have an area that acts as a pinboard, a place where children can add or remove notes, doodles, ideas and drawings. You could encourage this by giving them something to research that reflects the topic you are studying. Perhaps you are teaching 'festivals'; in this case ask them to research, draw and note down ideas about this topic. You will have an interesting display just from their doodles. Change this to complement what they are learning.

Book corners and shelves are, of course, an essential part of every classroom, but as well as filling the shelves with the most popular literature, have a look for books about interesting and inspiring people and places.

As a little girl, I stumbled upon a curiosity cabinet in the main hall of the junior section of my primary school. I can remember being so intrigued by what I saw. I'm not even sure if I understood what most of the interesting objects were, but nonetheless was totally and utterly enthralled. Tabletop displays are often popular with younger children but they can also be an amazing resource for older classes: there is nothing quite like handling artefacts first-hand. Ask children to use a logbook to write descriptions about what they find on the display table. Keep this book on the table even as displays change. It will prove an interesting and descriptive resource to reflect on during the last weeks of term.

Any classroom full of interesting, informative and well-presented activities, no matter how big or small, can become an inspiring learning environment. Classrooms should be welcoming environments that continue to make learning a positive and above all extremely happy experience for all.

Nathalie Frost, 2011

Bringing the Garden Inside

This section is designed to give any chosen area a fresh new look. By gleaning inspiration from the natural world, the children will be able to help transform parts of the school into unique and uplifting spaces. It is always good to begin with making drawings. Go outside to your garden area or visit a local park. Encourage the children to notice leaves, flowers and foliage.

A Mixed-media Masterpiece

Resources

- Large roll of thick paper or card (you can use plywood for a more permanent piece)
- Mixed fabrics (try to find a mixture of textures)
- Paint and brushes
- Paper and pencils
- Felt pens
- Scissors
- Glue
- Maps of the area
- Junk jewellery
- Shiny paper

Approach

1 Invite the children to paint the background with a blue sky, grass and trees.
2 Ask the children to make leaves for the trees by drawing on paper and painting on fabric.
3 Cut out the leaves and collage them onto the tree painting using glue.
4 Encourage the children to twist and scrunch paper and fabric to make flowers and stems.
5 Stick the flowers to the bottom of the picture to form a garden.
6 Embellish the work using copies of local maps so that the children can find where they live within the local area.
7 Use old bits of junk jewellery and shiny paper to decorate.
8 Ask the children to use a small brush to paint a row of people in the distance. Make these shapes simple as anything too complicated may deflect from the main aim of the picture, which is to create a stunning garden.

Luscious Leaves

Resources

- Card
- Scissors
- Paint and brushes
- Oil pastels
- Masking tape
- Wire

Approach

1 Cut leaf shapes out of white/green card.
2 Ask the children to paint/colour and decorate the leaves using different shades of green.
3 Wrap masking tape around a piece of wire until it's completely covered, then paint the tape brown. This will form a small branch.
4 Make four small holes down the middle of each leaf. Starting at the bottom, thread small pieces of wire, going in one hole then out the other. Make sure you leave a few inches of wire at the bottom of the leaf. When you reach the last hole, fold the wire back over the leaf to fasten it down.
5 Attach the leaves by winding the access wire at the bottom of each leaf to the branch.

A Leafy Painting

Resources

- Paper
- Oil pastels
- Felt pens
- Paint and brushes

Approach

1 Look at different bushes and leaves; notice how the leaves overlap each other.
2 Cover the paper with a drawing of leaves using oil pastels and felt pens.
3 Outline the leaves and add in further detail using paint.

Cross-curricular Links

- **Science** – Look at growth and how plants develop. Grow sunflowers and other plants and document their development. In autumn collect leaves to draw and paint, using a magnifying glass to study them closely.
- **Literacy** – Devise poems about growing plants and use the 'Luscious Leaves' to frame a display of their work.

7

Flowers and Foliage

William Morris (1834–1896) is a great example of an artist/designer who used flowers and foliage as inspiration for his work. Before you begin this activity it is a good idea to look at his work and samples of other wallpaper designs. Discuss colours and how the patterns repeat. A simple display can be made from cutting out swatches from sample wallpaper books and asking the children to make drawings of their favourite swatch.

Growing Wallpaper

Resources

- Paper, A4 and A3 size
- Paint and brushes
- Scissors
- Glue/Blu-Tack®
- Colour copier, scanner and printer
- Butterfly drawings/foliage

Approach

1 Ask the children to paint a flower on a small sheet of paper.
2 Cut out the flowers and stick them to an A3 piece of paper, overlapping to form a design (around ten or twelve flowers per sheet).
3 Colour-photocopy or scan and print the collage image as many times as desired.
4 Cut the collages out and paste them to the wall (use Blu-Tack® if you don't want a permanent display).
5 Use butterfly drawings and foliage to decorate.

Blooming Paintings

Resources

- Paper and pencils
- Paint and brushes
- Felt pens
- Oil pastels
- Images of gardens in bloom

Approach

1 Invite the children to draw a simple frame the size of their choice onto the paper.

2 Ask the children to paint a simple landscape scene (green field and sky) and leave the painting to dry.

3 While the paint is drying use felt pens and oil pastels to decorate the frame with images of all the creatures found in the garden. They may decide to just use one creature for their border; for example, a spidery frame will work very well in contrast to the landscape scene.

4 Show the children images of gardens in bloom, then use brightly coloured paint to fill the green field with different flowers.

5 Ask the children to write down words they associate with the images used in their painting, then display the words along with the cut-out creatures and flowers.

Cross-curricular Links

- **Geography** – Research different flowers and plants from different climates. Make paintings of these and display next to each other to show contrasting climates.

Louise Bourgeois Spiders

Louise Bourgeois (1911–2010) was a French-American artist who produced many large spider sculptures. Her largest sculpture of a spider is around nine metres tall. For all ages her work makes a fascinating starting point for studying minibeasts and other creatures.

Sculpting Spiders

Resources

- Pictures of Louise Bourgeois' spiders
- Paper and pens
- Card
- Scissors
- Wire
- Masking tape
- Bubble wrap
- Black acrylic paint
- Leaves and stones

Approach

1 Talk to the children about how spiders look. Show them images of Louise Bourgeois giant spider sculptures.
2 Ask the children to cover their paper in spider drawings in the style of the artist.
3 Cut eight pieces of card to resemble long, spindly legs. The length depends on how big you want the spiders to be.
4 Strengthen each leg by placing a piece of wire on it and then wrap in masking tape.
5 To make the body, scrunch up some bubble wrap and cover with masking tape.
6 Attach the legs to the body using tape.
7 Paint the whole spider with black acrylic paint.
8 Display the spiders among leaves and stones.

Spider Pictures

Resources

- Images of spider webs
- Coloured paper
- Paint (black, grey, silver, white)
- Black card
- Silver markers (white pencil will also work)

Approach

1 Look at images of spider webs and discuss how and why they are made.
2 Use the paint on the coloured paper to experiment with the pattern of a spider web.
3 Decorate strips of black card with the silver markers to form a frame for the paintings.

Silky Spiders

Resources

- Old silky scarves or pieces of patterned fabric
- Card/pieces of wood
- Newspaper
- Masking tape
- Paint and brushes
- Glue

Approach

1 Cover the card/wood with the fabric.
2 Scrunch up the newspaper to form the body of the spider and then cover with masking tape.
3 Twist eight pieces of newspaper into long 'legs', cover them with masking tape and attach to the main body of the spider.
4 Ask the children to paint the spiders.
5 Glue the spiders onto the fabric.

Cross-curricular Links

- **Literacy** – Many traditional rhymes mention spiders, for example 'Incy Wincy Spider' and 'Little Miss Muffet'. Ask the children to devise their own nursery rhymes based around spiders and then to illustrate their work.

11

Bird Baths

Many large gardens and parks have bird baths, bandstands and even ponds and fountains. Bird baths can attract many different species of birds. Show the children images of different parks and gardens with special features. If possible visit a garden or a park. Ask the children to design and make drawings of a garden with unique features.

A Bird Bath Design

Resources

- Images of bird baths
- Paper and pencils
- Card and scissors
- Paint and brushes
- Wire
- Glue
- Masking tape
- Rolled paper tube

Approach

1 Ask the children to draw the shape of a bird bath on card. (Supply them with images of a variety of designs.) Use pencil to draw out designs, and then paint the bird bath.

2 Invite the children to draw and paint birds; cut these out then attach the birds to the bird baths with wire.

3 Display the bird baths on a painted grass background. Use some of the birds as a border.

4 For a free-standing bird bath, attach it to a rolled paper tube.

A Bird Bath for Outside

Resources

- Paper and pencils
- Terracotta pots and saucers
- Water-resistant adhesive
- Undercoat paint
- Acrylic paint
- Acrylic varnish
- Brushes

Approach

1. Encourage the children to design a bird bath.
2. Stick the bottoms of two pots together, then attach a saucer to the top.
3. Prime the pots using the undercoat paint.
4. When dry, ask the children to draw their designs on the pots.
5. Paint and varnish.

Cross-curricular Links

- **Design and Technology** – Ask the children to design a product for feeding seeds to birds. Make posters and packaging to promote the product.
- **History** – Study ways of feeding creatures in the past. Look at images of horse troughs and discuss why they have been necessary throughout history.

13

Creating Creatures

Paper can be a great modelling resource when scrunched, manipulated and covered with masking tape. It offers us a chance to recycle and is a cheap, resourceful way to create unique sculptures and models for the classroom environment. Use old boxes as a starting point to decorate with creatures and foliage. These will make great tabletop displays that the children can keep adding to.

3D Garden Creatures

Resources

- Images of garden creatures
- Newspaper
- Masking tape
- Glue
- Paint and brushes
- Leaves for display

Approach

1 Look at images of different creatures found in the garden and discuss.
2 Scrunch up the newspaper to form the main part of the body and head.
3 Encourage the children to wrap masking tape around to cover the newspaper.
4 Make the legs in the same way, then attach them using tape or glue.
5 To make a squirrel's tail, make a roll of newspaper, squeeze and tape at one end, then trim the top down to resemble a bushy tail.
6 Attach the tail using glue. Paint the creature.
7 Make a large wall display of a suitable envbriment.
8 Make a garden area in front of the display to create an environment to place the creature in.

Paper Butterflies

Resources

- Images of butterflies
- Paint and brushes
- Paper and pencils
- Old magazines/wrapping paper
- Scissors
- Wire
- Vase of flowers

Approach

1 Show the children images of butterflies. Ask them to draw and paint their own.
2 Cut out butterfly shapes from old magazines and wrapping paper.
3 Fold each butterfly in half and cut small slits through which to thread the wire.
4 Place the butterflies in a vase of flowers to display.

A Foxy Box

Resources

- Images of foxes
- Box
- Card/paper
- Paint and brushes
- Glue

Approach

1 Discuss images of foxes. Investigate where they live.
2 Use two sides of the box to decorate with an urban environment such as houses, roads and pavements, and the other two sides to decorate with a rural country scene showing fields and greenery.
3 Ask the children to draw and paint images of a fox. Once these have dried, the children should decide which environment they live in and stick their fox onto the box.

Cross-curricular Links

- **Geography** – Investigate contrasting landscapes and make drawings. Display them side by side.

Out of this World – Space

Space and the universe have always made interesting topics for children to study. The fascination with the unknown can stimulate children's imaginations and help create exciting learning environments.

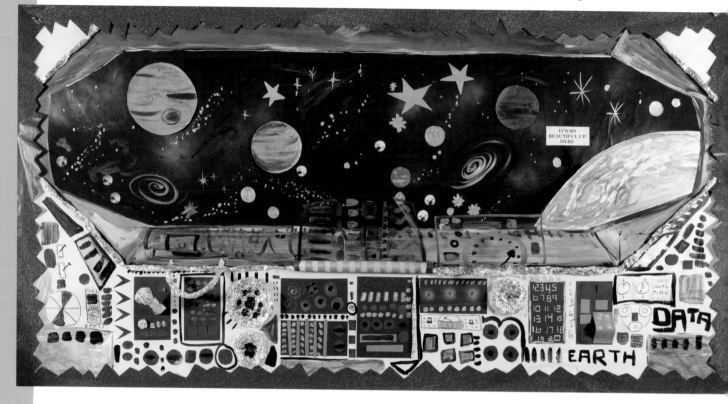

Rocket Cockpit Display

Resources

- Large black paper
- Paint and brushes
- Paper
- Scissors
- Card
- Shiny paper

Approach

1 Roll out a large, black piece of paper. Encourage the children to paint silver and white stars and galaxies.

2 Ask each child to paint their own control panel on paper. When they are dry, cut out and attach each picture to the bottom of the black, starry sky to create a busy control panel. Make some of their pictures 3D by using paper padding to form a relief.

3 Using large circles of card (of varying sizes), allow the children to paint the Earth, as well as other planets and the Moon, and attach them to the sky.

4 Either frame the painting with shiny paper or follow the activity on page 17 to make exciting buzzword borders.

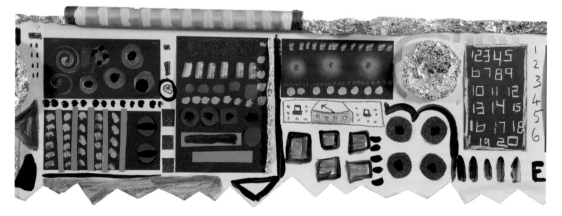

Space Words

There are many interesting and inspirational quotes made by astronauts from space to Earth and ground control. Neil Armstrong famously said, 'One small step for man, one giant leap for mankind.' The astronauts also reported, 'It's so beautiful up here,' referring to their landing on the Moon. The *Apollo 13* spaceship, which infamously struggled through its mission, reported, 'Houston, we have a problem.' These words can be used to embellish displays or make interesting works of art on their own when drawn and painted.

Resources

- Quotes from astronauts
- Pencils and pens
- Long strips of paper
- Paint and brushes
- Glue
- Glitter

Control Pad Models

Resources

- Shoebox lids
- Collage materials (eg bottle tops, tinfoil)
- Glue
- Paint and brushes
- Card
- Pens
- Scissors
- Split pins

Approach

1 Glue the collage materials to the inside of the shoebox lid to form the controls of the panel.
2 Paint and decorate.
3 Use pens and card to make dials. Cut out and attach using split pins so they can be turned.

Approach

1 Discuss with the children quotes made by astronauts about their space explorations.
2 Allow the children to devise their own sentences, imagining that they had experienced landing on the Moon.
3 Draw out the words in decorative writing on the long strips of paper.
4 Paint the words then decorate with glitter.
5 Display on their own or around a main display to form a frame.

Mystical Moon Face

Many people believe that they can see a face in the Moon. This activity will encourage the children to examine the surface of the Moon and experiment with using different materials to add textures to their artwork.

Resources

- Images of the Moon's surface
- Circles of card
- Foil
- Tissue paper
- Polystyrene balls
- Bubble wrap
- Paint and brushes
- Glitter
- Sand
- Glue and brushes

Approach

1 Look at images of the Moon's surface with the children. Ask them if they can see any faces. Discuss how it looks.

2 Give them each a piece of card and ask them to use foil and tissue to stick on craters and boulders.
3 Older children can be encouraged to sculpt a face to hide within their collage.
4 Encourage the children to use small polystyrene balls and cut-out pieces of bubble wrap to embellish their picture.
5 Use silver and grey paint to cover the collaged craters and boulders.
6 Add glitter and sand to give texture and sparkle to the Moon's surface.
7 Display all the Moon surface pictures next to each other.
8 Make some of the pictures stand out from the display by attaching a folded piece of firm card to the back and fixing this to the wall.

A Space at the Table

As well as making giant wall displays that help create inspiring learning environments, it is often some of the smaller, more intricate activities that can really stimulate children's imaginations. This works well as an individual project or team-building exercise.

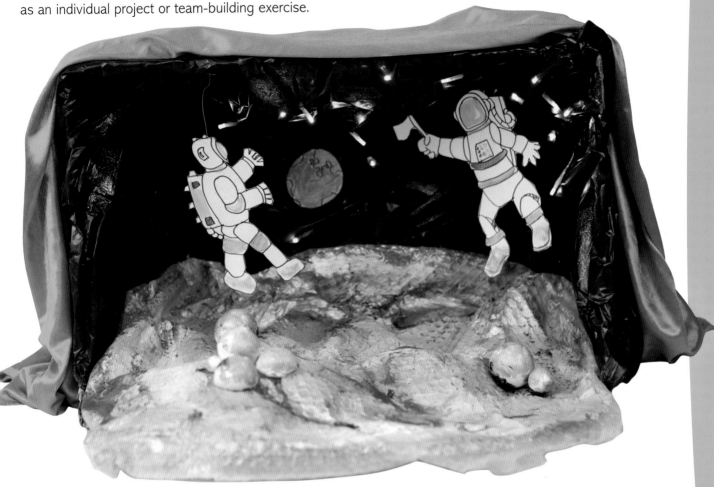

Resources

- Cardboard box
- Scissors
- Black bin bag
- Masking tape
- Battery-operated fairy lights (optional)
- Bubble wrap
- Glue
- Newspaper
- Small polystyrene balls
- Paint and brushes
- Silver glitter
- Card
- Pencils
- Cotton

Approach

1 Cut the front of the cardboard box to form your space ready to decorate.
2 Fill the back of the box with a black bin bag using masking tape. (Optional: attach the fairy lights to the back of the box to resemble the stars, feeding the lights through separate holes.)
3 Cover the base of the box with bubble wrap using glue, and pad using scrunched-up bits of newspaper.
4 Glue various polystyrene balls to the bubble wrap and paint the whole base using grey, white and silver paint. Then sprinkle on glitter.
5 Ask the children to draw spacemen and the Earth on card and cut out. Attach the Earth to the bin bag and hang the spacemen through the top using cotton.

The Moon

There have been many books with great illustrations showing the Moon and the planets. Please refer to *Zoo in the Sky* (Frances Lincoln, 1999) and *Once Upon a Starry Night* (Frances Lincoln, 2008), written by Jacqueline Mitton and illustrated by Christina Balit, for this activity. The illustrator uses beautiful, strong colours with interesting patterns to convey her interpretation of outer space. Discuss the illustrations with the children and ask them to think about how they could make their own individual images of space using unusual patterns and colour.

Fantasy Moon Paintings

Approach

1 Draw a frame to form a border. To form a frame, look at the illustrations and patterns found within the books. Ask the children to complete their own frames using paint.
2 In the centre of the picture draw planets and stars.
3 Use brightly coloured paint to make patterns on each of the planets and stars.
4 Use black and dark-blue paint to represent space. Paint swirling patterns on top of the black and blue paint.
5 Use iridescent craft paper to embellish the work.

Resources

- Copies of *Zoo in the Sky* and *Once Upon a Starry Night*
- Paper and pencils
- Paint and brushes
- Colourful, shiny craft paper

Moon Landing Collage

There are so many photos and articles about the Moon landings. An interesting activity is to ask the children to design their own headlines describing to the world the events of the Moon landing. Encourage them to imagine and discuss how they might feel if they were to do something extraordinary for the very first time, such as flying into space or landing on the Moon. Discuss how an important part of a journalist's work can be to create interesting and thought-provoking headlines for stories in newspapers. Talk about how it is possible to use just a few words to relay a groundbreaking story to a whole nation.

Resources

- Newspaper headlines
- Photos/drawings of the Moon landings
- Computer and printer
- Paper and pencils
- Felt/marker pens
- Card
- Scissors
- Glue

Approach

1 Ask the children to work on devising their own headlines illustrating the Moon landings, and to either write their words using bold markers or print them.
2 Cut up and collage the newspaper headlines onto a piece of card.
3 Encourage the children to use their own drawings of astronauts.
4 Draw stars and rockets to glue to the collage.
5 Use decorated zigzag card to form a frame.

Cross-curricular Links

- **Music** – Listen to Holst's *The Planets* and then encourage the children to use instruments to represent the sounds they might hear while walking on the Moon.

- **Literacy** – Ask the children to write letters to family and loved ones, imagining they are going to the Moon. Talk about how they would feel – their excitement and their anxieties.

The Victorians

The Victorians always seem to capture the imaginations of children. The way Victorian children were treated, their schooling, the workhouses and even the way they dressed always prove to be interesting areas of study. The Industrial Revolution (c1750–c1850) saw the invention of new machines capable of doing the jobs that had previously been done by hand. The whole period shows movement and change. In contrast to the sometimes bleak scenes of Victorian Britain, many

wealthy people lived very well, with servants and fine, decadent houses. There are many contrasting areas to look at that will make great starting points for works of art for the classroom.

A Victorian Scene – the Workhouse Gates

Resources

- Images of Victorian street scenes
- Sketchbooks and pencils
- Thick paper
- Paint and brushes
- Newspaper
- Scissors
- Cotton wool

Approach

1 Discuss how the streets of Victorian Britain may have looked. Look at the images.
2 Make sketches in sketchbooks and notes describing the atmosphere.
3 Give the children a sheet of thick paper and encourage them to mix up paint to form a smoggy sky at the top of the page. At the bottom scrunch up pieces of newspaper and attach to the paper.
4 On a separate sheet invite the children to draw their own street scene, showing working chimneys, stone and brick buildings, and workhouse gates.
5 Use paint to complete the scene.
6 When dry, cut out the street scene and attach it to the smoggy sky, painting over the scrunched-up paper to form a relief.
7 Use cotton wool to form smoke coming from the chimneys.
8 If possible display on a painted brick wall to form your Victorian environment.

Frivolous Victorian Cards

Victorian greetings cards were often very decorative and featured images of small children, Cupid, angels, flowers, lace and festive scenes. Because they are so busy and colourful they make a great activity for all ages and abilities as the children can collage as much or as little as they want. The cards will make a busy wall or tabletop display and are a great activity for Christmas.

Silhouette People

Resources

- Images of Victorian silhouette pictures
- Black card/paper
- Paper and pencils
- Scissors
- Glue
- Paint and brushes

Resources

- Images of old Victorian cards
- Card
- Paper and pencils
- Scissors
- Glue
- Scrap materials (old greetings cards, wrapping paper, ribbon, lace etc)
- Roll of paper (for tablecloth)
- Poster paints and brushes

Approach

1 Discuss the images of the cards.
2 Give the children a piece of card and ask them to fold it in half.
3 Ask the children to draw their own images: birds, flowers, ribbons etc.
4 Cut out the images, then arrange and stick onto a piece of card along with their choice of scrap material.
5 Ask the children to make the inside of their card. Encourage them to make this decorative with curly writing and illustrations.
6 Let the children paint a 'tablecloth' on the roll of paper using poster paints.
7 Display the cards on the hand-painted tablecloth to complete the whole display.

Approach

1 Ask the children to draw a silhouette of their neighbour, on black paper or card, or use images of Victorian silhouettes as a starting point. This should be a side profile.
2 Cut out the silhouette and attach it to a piece of oval-shaped plain paper.
3 Around the edge of the paper paint a wooden-style frame and decorate by drawing a pattern.
4 Display with Victorian-style picture bows.

Machine Power

Isambard Kingdom Brunel (1806–1859) was a leading engineer throughout the Industrial Revolution. He built bridges, tunnels and buildings, many of which are still in existence today. If you have access to the internet, search for the image of Brunel in front of giant chain links. Look at how big the links are in the image; it makes us wonder how large and powerful machines were becoming during this time.

Welcome to the Machine

Resources

- Images of Victorian machines
- Paper and pencils
- Card
- Paint and brushes
- Scissors
- Collage materials
- Glue

Approach

1. Ask the children to look at and discuss images of Victorian machines.
2. On paper and card, ask them to draw and paint cogs and wheels of different sizes.
3. Cut out the images and arrange them onto the wall. Make some of the cogs and wheels stand out by attaching a piece of card to the back of the image and then to the wall.
4. Paint collage materials and glue to the display.
5. This image can be worked on throughout the project by adding drawings and collage materials every few days.
6. Discuss what the children think the machine could be used for.

Ring My Bell

The Industrial Revolution was an important aspect of the Victorian era. People explored and developed inventions to make everyday living much easier and faster. The engineer Alexander Graham Bell (1847–1922) invented the telephone and was granted a patent for his design in 1876. The initial look of the telephone was basic, but soon the designs became more decorative and fancy.

Resources

- Card
- Small cuboid box
- Masking tape
- Pencils
- Paint and brushes
- Scissors
- String/wire

Approach

1. Fold a piece of thick card in half to form a tent shape and attach each side to the box using masking tape.
2. Encourage the children to think about how the receiver could be placed on top of the telephone. Use two Y-shaped pieces of card to attach to the top of the telephone model for the receiver to rest on.
3. To form the receiver ask the children to draw and paint the shape onto card and cut out.
4. The children can attach string or an old piece of wire to form the telephone cord.
5. Paint a dial and decorate the Victorian telephone.

Wrought-iron Gate and Fireplace

Resources

- Images of wrought-iron objects
- Paper and pencils
- Dark-coloured card
- Silver pens
- Paint and brushes
- Patterned paper

Approach

1. Talk with the children about things that were made from wrought iron during the Victorian era. Look at images and make sketches of gates and fireplaces.
2. Invite the children to use the silver pens and paint on the dark card to draw their gates and fireplaces.
3. Use patterned paper to collage tiles onto their fireplace drawings.

Large Victorian Display

This display can be as large or as small as you wish. It is a scene that could be added to throughout the topic. The important thing is to decide what areas you would like to include within the display and to work with groups of children to complete them. The display shows a contrast between the poor and the rich.

A Victorian Scene

Resources

- Images of Victorian scenes
- Paper and pencils
- Large pieces of card
- Paint and brushes
- Cotton wool
- Scissors
- Pens

Approach

1 Work with the children to paint grey buildings and wrought iron gates.
2 Another group could paint a smoggy sky and a steam train.
3 Work with a group of children to draw a Victorian house with plenty of windows and painted drapes on a large piece of grey card. To form a tiled, 3D staircase up to the house, fold a piece of card into step shapes. This can be attached to the base of the house. Add cotton wool for a smoke and smog effect.
4 Use black card to draw and cut out railings.
5 Ask the children to draw characters from Victorian times and place them onto the display. Make sure they think about how the character looks and whether they are poor or wealthy.
6 Surround the display with a frame made of smaller drawings on paper depicting gates.

Portrait of a Queen

Queen Victoria (1819–1901) had her portrait painted many times during her life. Images by different artists vary greatly. Thomas Sully's (1783–1872) portrait shows a young Queen Victoria going off to her coronation. She looks back to us, the viewers, as if saying goodbye to her past and preparing for her future as Queen of England. There are also photographs of Queen Victoria as an old lady.

2 Make drawings of the young Queen; use the same colours used in Sully's image.

3 Use cardboard to make a frame; then, using gold pens and paint, decorate the frame with patterns and words to describe how she may have felt during this part of her life.

4 Repeat the activity, this time looking at the images of the old Queen Victoria.

5 Display side by side on a roll of paper painted as if it were Victorian wallpaper.

6 You could also create a frame using fabric to represent expensive drapes.

Resources

- Copy of Thomas Sully's young Victoria and images of her as an old woman
- Paper and pencils
- Paint and brushes
- Cardboard
- Gold pens
- Roll of paper
- Fabric

Approach

1 Look at images of the painting of the young Queen. Notice the way she is facing. Talk about how she may have felt during this time. Then look at images of her as an older lady. Discuss the differences; as well as the obvious age difference ask the children how she may be feeling as an old lady reflecting on her reign and her life.

Cross-curricular Links

- **Science** – Explore different materials and their uses. Design gates from a variety of materials including wood, paper, card, strips of foil or polystyrene. Investigate which material is the strongest.
- **Literacy** – Ask the children to imagine and write about what life for the lower and upper classes would have been like. Compare and contrast the results. The work could be illustrated and then displayed side by side to show a stark contrast.

The Egyptians

Ancient Egyptian writing is known as hieroglyphics. The Egyptians used pictures to represent different objects, thoughts, ideas and people. There were more than 700 hieroglyphs. Sometimes pictures stood for whole words. The Egyptians painted hieroglyphics onto walls and carved them into stone, and these can still be seen today.

Hieroglyphics Display

Resources

- Books and images of hieroglyphics
- Paper and pencils
- Sugar paper/brown paper
- Paint and brushes
- Gold paper

Approach

1 Ask the children to look at and discuss the hieroglyphics. Talk about what they think they mean.

2 Make sketches and drawings of the hieroglyphics using what they see and inventing their own marks.
3 Ask the children to use paint to cover the sugar paper or brown paper with their hieroglyphics.
4 Let the children make smaller scrolls to decorate the border of the picture.
5 Make a frame for the picture using gold paper.
6 Surround the large picture with the individual scrolls.

create and display: Inspiring Learning Environments

Bubble Wrap Heads

There are so many fascinating characters which can be studied from the Ancient Egyptian period. A simple display can be made by collecting images of such characters and displaying them next to the children's sketches. As with many of the activities, we recycle as much as we can; in this case bubble wrap is used. Other materials such as newspaper and old plastic bags could be manipulated in the same way.

Resources

● Paper and pencils
● Bubble wrap
● Wide masking tape
● Paint and brushes

Approach

1 Let the children choose which character from Egyptian history they are going to create and encourage them to make some sketches.

2 Ask the children to manipulate the bubble wrap to form the basic shape of a head.
3 Fasten the bubble wrap in place using masking tape. Make sure all of their bubble wrap heads are covered in masking tape.
4 Ask the children to paint their heads and decorate.

Cross-curricular Links

● **Art and Design/History/Literacy** – Explore ancient texts and drawings such as cave paintings. Ask the children to develop their own drawings and marks to represent their own unique alphabet.
● **History** – Research the Rosetta Stone and find out why it was important in deciphering hieroglyphics.

Castles

Many castles were originally built from earth and timber and replaced later by stone. Castles were built as a form of safety and defence and often housed royalty. Ask the children to look at images of castles and compare them to the buildings we live in today.

A Castle Display

Resources

- Images of shields and coats of arms
- Paper and pencils
- Scissors
- Paints and brushes
- Roll of paper
- Sponges
- Card
- Masking tape
- Wire
- Pens

Approach

1 Encourage the children to look at images of shields and coats of arms. Ask them to design their own and decorate. These will be used later on to decorate the border.

2 Ask the children to paint the background of the display. Mix different shades of greens for the grass and blues for the sky. Flowers can then be painted on top.

3 Use a roll of paper to paint and print with sponges the grey bricks of the castle. Ask the children to help cut the castle out.

4 The children can roll up card to make the castle towers. A piece of card rolled into a cone shape big enough to cover the tower will make the perfect roof. Ask the children to attach these to the display using masking tape.

5 Assemble the display; a drawbridge can be added using card and wire.

6 Invite the children to draw and paint images of knights and soldiers. Use these to embellish the display where needed.

Drawbridges

Resources

- Cardboard boxes
- Acrylic paint and brushes
- Scissors
- Wire/string
- Interior design magazines
- Paper and pencils
- Glue
- Blue fabric

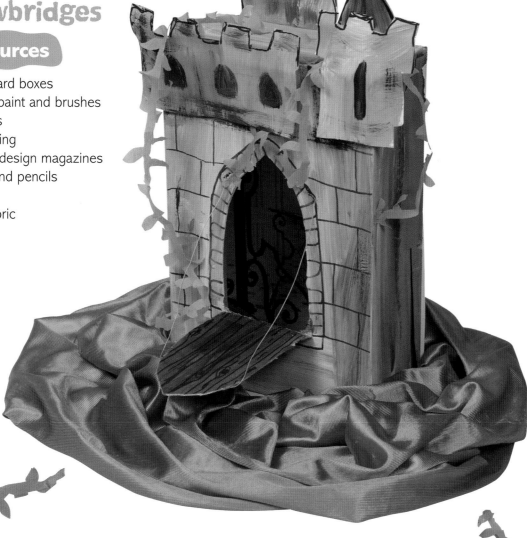

Approach

1 Ask the children to think about castles, drawbridges and moats.
2 Paint the boxes white and grey using acrylic paint.
3 Ask the children to think about stone buildings and encourage them to add detail to their castles, including a large front door.
4 Ask the children to cut the door around the top, leaving it attached to the box by the bottom so it opens and closes.
5 The children can then attach wire or string to the top of the door and the castle using small holes to feed it through. A knot in the wire/string will fasten it.
6 Ask the children to find a contemporary picture in an interior design magazine to use as the inside of their castle, or they can draw and colour their own. This can be cut to fit and stuck inside the box.

7 The blue fabric can be scrunched up around the castle to resemble a moat.

Cross-curricular Links

- **History/Geography** – Explore different bridge designs; investigate where they are found around the world. Research what materials were used in building these bridges.

Us and Them

The focus in this chapter is on individuality. A good starting point is to give the children small mirrors to explore their facial features. Encourage them to draw images of themselves, focusing on their eyes, nose, mouth and ears. These can be made into a display. The children can use magnifying glasses to examine their fingerprints. They can also use ink-pads to make prints of their fingerprints. Talk to the children about how unique everyone's fingerprints are, with no two individuals' ever being the same.

A Fingerprint Display

Resources

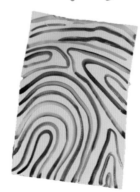

- A magnifying glass
- Paper and pencils
- Paint and brushes
- Scissors

Approach

1 Encourage the children to make drawings or sketches of the patterns they can see on their own fingers.
2 Ask them to paint simple paintings showing the patterns and lines. This is most effective using just a few colours.
3 Arrange their paintings on a display board, adding cut-out hand shapes.

Heads and Hearts

Resources

- Card/paper
- Scissors
- Computer and printer
- Glue

Approach

1 Ask the children to cut shapes of heads and hearts out of different coloured card/paper.

2 Encourage the children to think of words describing what they like to do or anything that's special to them. These can be typed on the computer, printed, and arranged within the heads and hearts.

Sweets   Football

My mum   Chocolate

Thoughts and Feelings

Many people choose to write diaries about themselves and their experiences. A great way for children to explore and find out about themselves is for them to draw and paint words that they associate with who they are and what they are like.

Word Paintings

Resources

- Paper and pencils
- Paint and brushes
- Tissue paper

Approach

1 Encourage the children to think about words that best describe their personalities.

2 Ask the children to write these down.
3 On a separate piece of paper the children can paint a background using their favourite colours. They should think carefully about mixing colours and use different brushstrokes.
4 Once the background is dry the children can paint their chosen words on top to finish their paintings.
5 Decorate with stars and doodles.
6 Use scrunched-up tissue paper to form a frame.

Memory and Thought Boxes

We can build up visual pictures by collecting items that we like and that have meaning for us. Joseph Cornell (1903–1972) was an American artist who collected memorabilia from junk shops and markets. These were placed inside boxes and displayed as pieces of art. Look at images of Joseph Cornell's work and ask the children to think about items they could display in their own boxes.

Resources

- Small objects of interest to the children
- Cardboard boxes
- Card
- Scissors
- Masking tape
- Pieces of wallpaper
- Magazines
- Paint and brushes

Approach

1 The children should think about which objects describe their interests (a shell from the beach, a painted football, etc).
2 The children can divide their boxes into sections ('shelves') using strips of card fastened using masking tape.
3 Ask the children to decorate the walls of their sections using old wallpaper, patterns from magazines and paint.
4 When the boxes are dry the children can place the items onto the shelves.

Tokens of Love and Friendship

Research the Foundling Museum, London, with the children and the story of the Foundling Hospital, which was London's first home for abandoned children.

The museum displays items which were left by mothers as tokens of love and to help them to identify their child should they return to collect them.

Resources

- Images of tokens from the Foundling Museum
- Paper and pens
- Collage material
- Small everyday objects
- Shoebox lids

Approach

1 Look at images of the tokens left by the mothers of the children.
2 Ask the children to design and make their own tiny tokens that they would leave with someone they care about. You could also add simple everyday objects such as keys or ribbons.
3 Display their tokens side by side in a decorated shoebox lid.

Phrenology

Phrenology is the study of the relationship between a person's character and the shape of their skull. There are many examples of ceramic 3D models depicting phrenology. Research images of these and get the children to draw their own. The children can think about words that best describe themselves and use these in their designs.

Phrenology Display

Resources

- Card
- Pencils
- Marker pens
- Paint and brushes
- A collection of different images and patterns (old musical scores, sporting images, wallpaper)
- Glue

Approach

1 Ask the children to help draw a shape of a head on card using pencil. Once they are happy with the shape they can go over it using marker pens.
2 The head can be painted with skin colours. The features can then be added on top.
3 The children can help divide the head into sections using a marker pen.
4 Each section can be decorated to represent a different section of the brain. For example, one section could be covered in musical scores to show that the person is musical, or with an image of a football pitch to show that the person is sporty.

5 Patterns and decoration can be added to the sections.
6 Ask the children to think of words they associate with each section.
7 The children can now add sections around the head, making sure they leave enough space to add the words of their choice.

Phrenology Models

Resources

- Card
- Scissors
- Marker pens
- Collage material
- Gold/silver pens
- Glue
- Masking tape

Approach

1 Ask the children to cut out a head shape from two pieces of card held together. These will form the front and back of the models.
2 The children should then divide both sides of the head into a few sections using marker pen.
3 Ask the children to really think carefully about how they feel and what inspires them in and out of school. Tell them the model should reflect themselves and incorporate their memories, interests and skills.
4 Each section should be decorated using collage material or gold/silver pens to make them really stand out.
5 The children can attach the two sides of the head together using a tube of card with masking tape. The tube should act as support and help stand the model up.

Cross-curricular Links

- **Science/History** – Research historical cures for human ailments and the methods used.

The Senses

Encourage the children to collect items and artefacts that stimulate each sense to make a tabletop display. Include items such as flowers, perfume, stone, silk, sand, musical instruments and recordings of different sounds. Keep a sense diary on the table with the artefacts so the children can make notes about each item and which sense they stimulate.

The Wheel of Sense

Resources

- Card
- Pencils
- Pens
- Collage material including sweets, pasta, etc
- Sense-stimulating items, eg flowers, silk
- Scissors
- Glue

Approach

1 Draw a circle on a piece of card and divide it into five sections. Label each section with a different sense.

2 Ask the children to draw and collage in each section using the appropriate materials for each sense.

3 Ask the children to draw noses, eyes, ears, mouths and hands. These can be cut out and added to make an interesting border.

Smoothie Bar

This can be made as a simple wall display, or a whole corner of the classroom can be transformed. It provides an exciting way for the children to study fruits and vegetables, and to explore their properties.

Resources

- Paper and pencils
- Coloured pens
- Paint and brushes
- Scissors
- Coloured card
- Straws

Approach

1 Ask the children to think about fruit and vegetables. Do they like them? Which is their favourite/least favourite? and so on.
2 Encourage the children to draw smoothies using a variety of colours. They should think about the flavours of their smoothies and choose the colours accordingly.
3 The children should also make labels for the drinks. These can be printed from a computer or made by hand. They can then be cut out and stuck to their smoothies.
4 Encourage the children to draw and colour different fruits and vegetables that can be added to the smoothie bar.
5 Back the display board using a plain, light colour. This will act as the inside of the smoothie bar. Use strips of card to represent shelves.
6 Attach the children's smoothies onto the display. Straws and labels can be added too.

Smoothie of the Day

Resources

- Recipe cards/books
- Computer
- Paper and pencils
- Coloured paper
- Glue
- Pens
- Collage materials
- Scissors

Approach

1 Ask the children to look at recipe cards/books or use the computer to research and note down the ingredients used in making a smoothie.
2 Encourage the children to use coloured paper and collage to represent their favourite smoothie.
3 Ask the children to write out their recipe, which could then be displayed with their smoothie.

Cross-curricular Links

- **Science** – Ask the children to design their own healthy smoothie recipe using a few of their favourite fruits and vegetables. Explore the children's knowledge of the names of different fruits and vegetables and their health benefits.

Dinosaurs

The study of dinosaurs appeals to all ages. Visually they make a great starting point for giant displays. Look at images of fossils with the children and make sketchbook drawings. Mary Anning (1799–1847) was famous for her fossil findings. She came from Lyme Regis, a coastal town in the south of England where she opened a shop selling the fossils she found in the area. Mary Anning made many important finds that contributed to the scientific thinking about prehistoric life.

Mary Anning's Fossil Shop

Look at images and discuss what Mary Anning would have sold. Talk about what would be fun to make for a classroom fossil shop. Make drawings in sketchbooks planning the shop.

Resources

- Images of fossils
- Paper and pencils
- Scissors
- Paint and brushes
- Tissue paper
- Glue
- Card
- Images of Mary Anning

Approach

1 Ask the children to draw and cut out images of fossils.
2 Use scrunched-up painted paper to make rocks and stones.
3 Invite the children to scrunch up long pieces of tissue paper and stick in a spiral shape to form ammonite fossils.
4 Fold and attach card to the wall to form shelves for displaying the children's drawings and models of fossils.
5 Ask the children to draw a picture of Mary Anning's head wearing a bonnet.
6 Use tissue paper for her long green outfit, fixing it to the wall, then attach the head.
7 Make signs describing what is sold in the shop.
8 If possible place a table under the display; invite children to arrange their paper models of stones, rocks and fossils. Make labels and price tags for these.

Mary Anning Posters

Ask the children how they think people advertise their shops and businesses today. Discuss how Mary Anning may have advertised her fossil shop. Compare the two.

Resources

- Posters and advertisements
- Paper and pencils
- Paint and brushes

Approach

1 Look at posters and advertising material with the children.
2 The children can create their own posters using bold, simple text.
3 Encourage the children to use colour to embellish their posters.

Cross-curricular Links

- **Literacy** – Recite the tongue-twister 'She sells seashells on the seashore'. Ask the children to experiment and invent their own tongue-twisters.
- **Design Technology** – Design boxes and bags for the fossils bought from the shop.

- **Geography** – Ask the children to research into where fossils and dinosaur bones have been discovered. They can make a note of this in their own dinosaur journal.

Fossils

Discuss with the children what novelty gifts could be sold in their class fossil shop – ammonite-shaped lollipops, speckled dinosaur eggs, fossil-shaped cookies, for example. Ask children to design the things that they would like to have in the shop. Use these drawings to make an interesting display. An extension of this would be to try to make some of their designs.

Clay Fossils

Resources

- Images of fossils/real fossils
- Self-hardening clay
- Clay tools
- Paint and brushes
- Fine glitter
- Varnish
- Sand

Approach

1 Look at images of fossils, or some real fossils if available.
2 Use the clay to mould into fossil shapes. Encourage the children to design their own.
3 When the models are dry, paint, sprinkle with glitter and then varnish.
4 Use sand to sprinkle over the fossils and display.

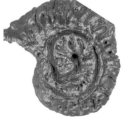

Chocolate Footprints

Resources

- Images of dinosaur footprints
- Slabs of chocolate
- Clay tools
- Icing sugar, edible glitter and cocoa powder

Approach

1 Ask the children to refer to the images of dinosaur footprints.
2 Encourage them to scrape and dig their own dinosaur footprint shape into the flat side of a bar of chocolate.
3 Decorate with edible glitter, icing sugar and cocoa powder.

create and display: *Inspiring Learning Environments*

Fossil Collage Display

Ammonites existed within interesting spiral-shaped shells. Images of these fossils make an exciting display. The children can design different sized ammonites, as archaeological findings show that these creatures varied in size.

Resources

- Card
- Pencils
- Oil pastels
- Pens
- Paint and brushes
- Scissors
- Masking tape
- Coloured paper
- Staples/drawing pins

Approach

1 Encourage the children to look at fossils and choose appropriate coloured card to use for their designs.

2 Ask the children to draw fossils and embellish them with oil pastels, pens and paints.

3 Ask the children to carefully cut out their designs ready to be displayed.

4 To make some of the fossils 3D on the display the children can attach rolled-up pieces of card to the backs of their designs. These can be fastened with masking tape.

5 Use coloured paper to back the display board and start to arrange the children's fossils. The 3D fossils can be attached using staples or drawing pins through the tubes of card on the back.

Fantastic Jurassic

Creating a dinosaur landscape can be a great art activity for all ages. Ask the children to think about and draw pictures of what they believe the world would have looked like when dinosaurs existed. Encourage the class to be as adventurous as they can and allow their imaginations to run wild while making their drawings.

Dinosaur World

Resources

- Paint and brushes
- Long roll of paper
- Pencils
- Scissors
- Card

Approach

1 Roll out the long piece of paper and ask the children to draw the kinds of huge flowers, trees and patterns that may have been found in a prehistoric environment using pencil.

2 Ask the children to help mix different shades of reds, yellows, blues, pinks and greens.

3 Encourage the children to paint the flowers and patterns and all the spaces between until the whole piece of paper is covered.

4 Ask the children to cut out the flowers and shapes.

5 Start to arrange their work onto the display. If the children want to they can add dinosaur heads creeping through the trees. Extend the display onto a table. (NB Rolled-up tubes of card attached to the back of the children's figures make perfect stands.)

Dinosaur Model

Resources

- Images of dinosaurs
- Newspaper
- Wide masking tape
- Paint and brushes
- Paper and pencils

Approach

1 Encourage the children to look at the particular dinosaur you are all going to make and ask them to create some drawings.
2 The children can start scrunching, rolling and taping together the newspaper until the basic shape of the body is complete.
3 Using the same method, the legs, arms and tail can be attached.
4 Ask the children to cover the dinosaur in tape until there is no newspaper showing.
5 Encourage the children to look at different shades of green and ask them to mix them. They can start to paint one side of the dinosaur with all the different shades. Once one side is dry the other can be painted in the same way.
6 The children can add eyes, nose, teeth and claws to finish.

Dinosaur Teeth and Eyes Display

Resources

- Images of dinosaurs
- Paper and pencils
- Felts and crayons
- Scissors
- Card

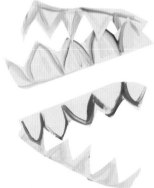

Approach

1 Ask the children to look at images of dinosaurs.
2 Encourage them to design lots of different sized dinosaur eyes. They can colour these using reds, yellows and black.
3 Ask the children to cut out their designs.
4 The dinosaur jaws can be made in two parts. Ask the children to cut out the top and bottom jaws from white card.
5 Arrange the children's work onto the display board making some of the eyes and teeth stand out using rolled-up pieces of card.

45

Greek Myths and Legends

The myths and legends of Ancient Greece include many exciting tales that children love to read and hear. The fantastic characters conjured up by the stories also create ideal opportunities for display.

A Magical Dolphin Wall

The dolphin features in many designs within Greek art. The dolphin mural at Knossos in Crete is probably the most famous. In certain myths and legends dolphins are seen to help and even rescue people. Read the tale of *Arion and the Dolphin* (Orion Childrens, 1997) as a starting point.

Resources

- Images of dolphins and the mural from Crete
- Large piece of paper
- Paint and brushes
- Paper and pencils
- Oil pastels
- Scissors
- Newspaper
- Masking tape
- Shiny paper

Approach

1 Use a selection of different blue paints to form the sea. Make wavy marks to represent water.
2 Use oil pastels to draw dolphins and fish. Encourage the children to use paint as well as oil pastels, and when dry, cut out the images.
3 Once it is dry, attach the 'sea' to the wall and display the dolphins by padding them out with newspaper using masking tape and covering it over with the dolphin paintings to give a 3D effect.
4 Use shiny paper to embellish the display.
5 Frame the display with Greek-style patterns.

Greek Dolphin and Patterns

A popular pattern in Greek art is the 'key' and it is used to decorate many pots and vases. Its name comes from the square pieces sticking out in the pattern that look rather like a key. The pattern is a continuous one that meanders and keeps turning on itself. Combined with the image of the dolphin, this will make beautiful, decorative works of art.

Resources

- Images of Greek patterns and dolphins
- Card
- Paper and pencils
- Scissors
- Paint and brushes

Approach

1 Ask the children to draw on card the shape of an ancient Greek vase or plate.
2 Cut out the image and then decorate with Greek-style patterns by drawing and painting.
3 Display the images together and frame with a Greek-style border, which the children can draw or paint on paper.

A Paper Dolphin Mosaic

The Greeks developed many different ways of creating images, mosaic being a very popular method.

Resources

- A variety of colourful card or thick paper
- Pencils
- Scissors
- Glue

Approach

1 Discuss mosaics and how they were made.
2 Ask the children to draw a simple dolphin shape on a piece of card.
3 Encourage the children to cut out small shapes to form the mosaic tiles.
4 Ask the children to stick the pieces of card/paper onto the dolphin picture, remembering to leave spaces between each piece to give the effect of a mosaic.

47

The Story of Icarus

Icarus is a well-known character from Greek mythology. He became imprisoned with his father Daedalus and they strove to think of ways to escape. They watched the birds flying, were struck by how free they were and decided to escape by making wings for themselves using feathers and wax. Icarus became overexcited and flew too close to the Sun, resulting in the wax melting. The story of Icarus and his melting wings has fascinated children for years. It contains strong messages about keeping safe from danger.

Icarus Feathers and Wings Display

Resources

- The story of Icarus
- Red, yellow, black and orange card
- Scissors
- Paper and pencils
- Paint and brushes
- Shiny paper

Approach

1 Ask the children to cut out leaf shapes from coloured card.

2 Encourage the children to cut slits around the edges of the leaves and ruffle them to turn them into feathers.
3 Ask the children to draw and cut out an image of Icarus. They can also paint a yellow sun.
4 Arrange Icarus onto the display board leaving plenty of room for his feathers.
5 Start to position the feathers around his arms. Ensure that some stick out of the display for added effect.
6 The children's feathers can also be used as a border, making sure that each one overlaps the next.
7 Ask the children to cut out letters from shiny paper for the Icarus display title.

Icarus Sun Paintings

As well as making a communal display the class can enjoy making individual Icarus works of art. These pictures can be as small or as large as you want them to be. In the example, yellow paint has been used, but to give a stronger impact encourage the children to experiment with gold paper and glitter to collage onto the sun. Ask them to think of ways to make their sun images 3D.

Resources

- White, yellow, red, black and orange card
- Blue, yellow and orange paint
- Brushes
- Scissors
- Glue

4 Encourage the children to cut leaf shapes from coloured card. These shapes can easily be turned into feathers by cutting slits around the edges and ruffling up.

5 The children can arrange the feathers around their pictures to form a border.

Approach

1 Ask the children to paint a sun using yellows and oranges on white card.

2 Ask the children to use light shades of blue to paint the sky.

3 From a piece of black card the children can cut out a silhouette of Icarus to add to their picture.

49

Theseus and the Minotaur

The story of Theseus and the Minotaur is an exciting myth from Greek history. The Minotaur was a monster at the centre of a huge maze on the island of Crete. The son of the king of Athens, Theseus, went in search of the Minotaur to end the terror the beast was causing, using string to find his way back through the maze.

The Minotaur Display

Resources

- Story of Theseus and the Minotaur
- Brown, white and grey sugar paper
- Pencils
- Paint and brushes
- Oil pastels
- Scissors
- Roll of white paper
- Green material/plastic vines

Approach

1 Read the story of Theseus and the Minotaur to the class. Encourage the children to think about the story and discuss what the Minotaur may have looked like.

2 Ask the children to draw their Minotaur heads on the sugar paper and use paint or oil pastels to decorate. These can then be cut out.

3 Encourage the children to research Ancient Greek patterns. They can start painting the patterns onto the roll of paper. Once these are dry they can be cut into wide strips to use as the border of the display.

4 Ask the children to design and paint the 'Minotaur' sign. This can be attached to the middle of the display board.

5 Arrange the children's Minotaur heads around the sign. These can be made to stand out of the display for added effect.

6 Arrange the green material/plastic vine in or around the display.

create and display: Inspiring Learning Environments

The Minotaur's Amazing Maze Model

Resources

- Card
- Pencils
- Scissors
- Glue
- Paint and brushes

Approach

1 Ask the children to mark a start and a finish to their maze on a piece of card.
2 Encourage the children to create parts of their maze by using strips of card. The strips should be folded twice lengthways so each path has two walls, then glued to the card.
3 The children can start arranging the maze walls. They can add different paths by cutting into the wall of another to join them together. They can cut and fold the ends of the paths to make a dead end when they need to.
4 Once the path from start to finish is complete the children can add more paths.
5 The spaces between the paths can be painted using greens or browns. Greek patterns can be added too.

A Minotaur Model

Resources

- Images of the Minotaur
- Paper and pencils
- Card
- Scissors
- Paint and brushes
- Carboard box
- Glue
- Fabric

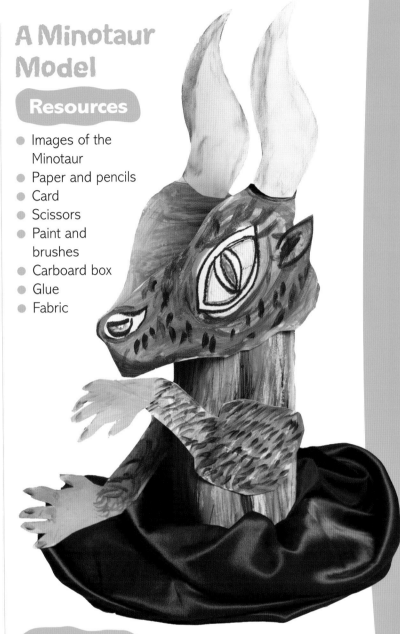

Approach

1 Look at images of the Minotaur and make sketches of him. Encourage the children to develop their own ideas of what he may have looked like.
2 Draw out the side of the Minotaur's head on a piece of folded card and cut this out – this will give the children both sides of his head.
3 Ask the children to paint the sides, with marks to represent fur.
4 Make horns from white card and attach to each side of the head.
5 Paint the box, and when dry attach each side of the Minotaur head to each side of the box.
6 Draw two huge eyes, cut out and attach.
7 Display with a piece of fabric at the base of the box.

Medusa

Medusa is a frightening character from Greek mythology. She was an innocent young girl until she took her friend into the temple of the goddess Athena. Athena looked down upon Medusa from the sky and was very angry that she had trespassed. She turned Medusa into an ugly woman with snakes for hair. If anybody looked at her they would turn into stone statues for ever.

A Head of Snakes Display

Resources

- The story of Medusa
- Paper and pencils
- White card
- Oil pastels
- Paint and brushes
- Images of Greek architecture
- Scissors

Approach

1 Ask the children to start by drawing snakes in rows on sheets of white card. These can be decorated using oil pastels. Paint can be added on top to bring the pastel colours out.

2 Ask the children to help to draw the head of Medusa. The children can then paint Medusa.

3 Encourage the children to look at images of Greek architecture to get ideas about patterns and colours. Ask the children to draw and paint Greek pillars and statues for the border of the display. The children can also paint Greek-style patterns onto paper.

4 Arrange Medusa on the display board and attach each snake to her head. These can be sticking out of the display to bring them to life. Attach the pillars and statues around Medusa and arrange the Greek patterned paper in the spaces.

Medusa Model

Resources

- Paper and pencils
- Card
- Paint and brushes
- Newspaper
- Masking tape
- Scissors
- Stapler

Approach

1 Ask the children to draw and paint snakes on a piece of card or paper.
2 The children can scrunch up pieces of newspaper to create the head of Medusa, which can be fastened and covered with masking tape.
3 The children can now attach the snakes to their Medusa models. Encourage the children to think about which colours to paint their models.
4 To make the models stand up, a base can be made out of two pieces of card. This can be stapled together at both sides, leaving a gap into which the head can be placed.

Medusa Hat

Resources

- Card
- Pencils
- Paint and brushes
- Scissors
- Stapler
- Glue

Approach

1 Ask the children to start to design their hats on wide strips of card. Greek patterns can be added along with snakes.
2 Ask the children to draw and paint snakes on a separate piece of card. These can be cut out and attached to their hats. This can be done using staples or glue.
3 Help the children to mark the size of their hats by fitting them around their head; when the size has been marked the hat can be taken off and stapled together.

Story Corners

Story corners for young children should be full of inspiring images and words. The displays in this section would be particularly suitable for the Early Years and Key Stage 1. Whether these are on the wall, on a desktop, a shelf or dangling like a mobile from the ceiling, the aim is to make the area as inspirational as possible. There are so many different and beautiful stories from the past and present that it can be quite a task to choose just one if you are considering making a display area based on these tales. Decide which genre you are going to focus on and build up your characters and buzzwords surrounding this. The Brothers Grimm, Roald Dahl, fairy tales and classic tales all make excellent starting points for your inspiring learning environment.

Story Corner Design

Resources

- Images of story characters
- Paper and pencils
- Oil pastels, felt pens
- Paint and brushes
- Colourful paper
- Scissors
- Mixed materials (eg straw, fabric)

Approach

1 Spend time with the children deciding which stories and characters they would like to feature in the display.

2 Work with the children to draw and paint or colour a picture representing the story/stories.
3 Cover the display board with paper and paint a simple giant book.
4 Cut out and add the characters to the board.
5 Use real materials if possible: for example, straw for the three little pigs or a red piece of fabric for a cloak.
6 Display the images side by side and overlapping.
7 Ask the children to cut out small book shapes to form frames. They could decorate these with images of their favourite story.

Cinderella's Ball Gown and Slipper

Using real artefacts as your base for displaying children's work is an exciting way to stimulate their interest in reading and a good way to recycle unwanted items.

Resources

- Old party dress
- Old shoe/slipper
- Thick paper or card
- Pencils
- Felt pens
- Oil pastels
- Computer and printer
- Velcro or masking tape

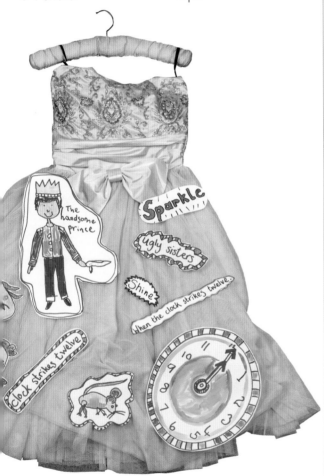

Approach

1 Invite the children to draw and colour characters or artefacts from the story.
2 Ask them to write or print out words and sentences from the story.
3 Attach their work to the old party dress and place some of the words in and around the shoe/slipper, then display in the classroom.

The Three Bears' Bowls

Resources

- Old plastic or paper bowls
- Acrylic paint
- Brushes
- Paper and pencils
- Felt pens
- Oil pastels
- Scissors
- Sponges

Approach

1 Paint the bowls with patterns and images from the story.
2 Invite the children to write words and sentences from the story and to decorate them.
3 Cut out the words and display them around the bowls.
4 Use sponges to paint a tablecloth to display the bowls on.

Encourage the children to think about stories and what happens in them, and to collect artefacts that give people clues about what their favourite story may be.

55

Classic Tales

The latter part of the junior years should be just as full of visual stimulation regarding stories as the earlier years at school. A multi-character display with clues and information will appeal to all abilities. The display can be ongoing throughout the year, with characters coming and going as the children discover them and their story. The images will evolve just as they do with young readers.

Classic Stories

Resources

- A range of classic texts
- Paper and pencils
- Paint and brushes
- Pens
- Scissors
- Old books (ready for recycling)
- Shiny paper

Approach

1 Encourage the children to think about their favourite stories, to make notes and to write about their favourite sections of the book.
2 Ask them to draw and paint something associated with their story. It may be a character or a place.
3 Cut out the images and display side by side.
4 Invite the children to write buzzwords and questions to place around the story display.
5 Use pages from old books to decorate the display.
6 Form a border from elaborate shiny paper to symbolise the importance and beauty of reading.

A Painted Bookshelf

Resources

- Paper and pencils
- Gold and silver markers
- Paint and brushes

Approach

1 Ask the children to research stories and their authors. Encourage them to make a list of their favourite stories and who wrote them.

2 Invite the children to draw the spines of their books as they would appear on a shelf.

3 Paint the books, and when dry ask them to write the name of the author and the text on the spines using gold and silver markers.

4 Display the painted bookshelves next to each other around the room to form long, interesting shelves.

5 Alternatively display as a pile of books (as above) if you don't have enough space.

Bookworms

Resources

- Card
- Pencils
- Felt pens
- Synopses of different texts
- Chalk
- Scissors

Approach

1 Ask the children to draw out long, wriggly worms on card.

2 Look at synopses of different texts with the children, then encourage them to write their own synopsis of a different story on the body of the worms.

3 Colour around the worms using felt pens and chalk.

4 Display the worms creeping around cut-out books.

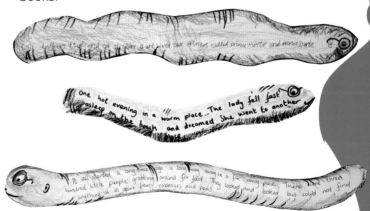

57

Travel

Through creating this display the children can learn about different modes of transport. The class can discuss how many different ways there are to travel, then talk about how they each travel to school and which transportation they have used in the past. Ask the children to write down as many modes of transport as they can before you begin the display.

Travel Display

Resources

- Roll of paper
- Paint and brushes
- Tissue/crêpe paper
- Card
- Scissors
- Pencils
- Old map or atlas
- Stapler
- Glue

Approach

1 Stretch out a roll of paper and ask the children to paint in the hills using different shades of green. The river or sea needs to be along the bottom and painted using different shades of blue. The sky can be added in the same way with different shades. Tissue paper, when scrunched, makes a great wave-like texture. This can be stapled or stuck on afterwards.

2 Discuss with the children the different kinds of roads and their uses. Roads can be cut out of card to fit over and around the hills. White road markings and lines can be added with paint.

3 Ask the children to draw and paint different types of transport on separate card, including planes, cars, trains, bicycles, boats, hot-air balloons, skateboards and so on. These can be cut out and added later.

4 The children can paint flowers, train tracks and clouds.

5 Arrange the children's drawings onto the display.

6 The children can gently tear the pages out of the old atlas or map book. These can be added around the display to make an interesting border.

Tickets and Passport Display

Resources

- Used travel tickets
- Computer and printer
- Travel symbols
- Pencils
- Card/paper
- Paint and brushes
- Oil pastels
- Scissors

Approach

1 Encourage the children to look at and bring in old travel tickets. These could be from buses, trains, planes or even funfair tickets. The children can also research what a passport looks like and print images from the computer.

2 Ask the children to print small pictures of planes, buses or any travel symbols. They can design their own too.

3 The children can draw and paint their tickets and passports on a piece of card or paper. They can then cut out their travel symbols and add these appropriately.

4 Arrange their passports and tickets onto the display board. Surround the display with a frame made up of words connected with travel: for example, 'destination', 'arrival', 'country', 'nationality', 'currency', 'language' and 'luggage'.

Cross-curricular Links

- **History** – Explore modes of transport from the past. Make a picture depicting transport from the past. Include penny-farthings, horse-drawn carriages and hovercrafts.
- **PE/Music** – Listen to different pieces of music and songs that mention travelling and devise movements to accompany these.

Colour and Shape

The French artist Henri Matisse (1869–1954) produced many amazing works in his lifetime. He was interested in colour and how we respond to it. He was a member of the Fauve movement, 'Fauve' meaning 'wild beast', and the artists during this period weren't frightened of using and exploring all colours. His work is always popular in the classroom as he used so many bold, simple shapes. Look at images from his collage period and his pictures of dancers.

A Matisse Shape Collage

Resources

- Images of work by Matisse
- Paper
- Brightly coloured paints
- Brushes
- Scissors
- Oil pastels
- Large sheet or roll of paper
- Glue

Approach

1 Look at and discuss images of work by Henri Matisse. *La Gerbe* is an interesting image as it is full of simple painted pieces of paper that Matisse has collaged onto a plain background.

2 Ask the children to paint and cut out simple shapes in the style of Matisse.

3 While these are drying use oil pastels and paint to form a background on the large sheet of paper.

4 Arrange the shapes from point 2 onto the brightly coloured surface, then stick down to form a stunning Matisse-style panel.

create and display: Inspiring Learning Environments

Matisse Figures

As well as being interested in colour, Matisse was intrigued by movement. His pictures are often musical and he depicts huge figures dancing around within his work.

Find images of Matisse's dancers. He created these in collage and in paint.

Resources

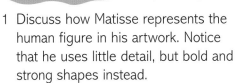

- Images of works by Matisse
- Roll or large piece of paper
- Oil pastels
- Brightly coloured paint
- Brushes
- Simple image of a figure dancing
- Paper and pencils
- Scissors
- Glue

Approach

1 Discuss how Matisse represents the human figure in his artwork. Notice that he uses little detail, but bold and strong shapes instead.

2 As in the previous activity, create a stunning background by splitting the paper into sections and using oil pastels and brightly coloured paint to fill each. Encourage the children to experiment with making different marks with their oil pastels, then to paint on top. This should create an interesting effect.

3 Invite the children to draw and cut out simple, bold dancing figures; arrange these on the colourful background. Ask them to decorate the background with cut-out drawings of hearts, leaves, musical notes and stars.

4 Use painted strips of paper to form frames.

Cross-curricular Links

- **MFL** – Find out the French words for the shapes used in the images, then write or print them out and label the picture.

- **Geography/Art** – Look at Matisse's work from his time spent in Nice. Discover what the climate is like. Find out about other artists from different parts of the world.

- **Science** – Discuss movement and joints within the human body. Make drawings of these and label them. Use split pins and card to construct moving joints.

Weather

Different weather conditions will make interesting starting points for a variety of displays. Creating a changeable weather corner in the classroom can be an exciting way to form an inspiring learning environment. A 'Sunshine Corner' could be bright and colourful, with images and information about warm places. A 'Watery Wet Corner' could contain images by artists such as JMW Turner (1775–1851), who spent his life painting and observing different weather conditions. The important thing is that whatever you choose, fill it with different ways of looking at the weather: reports, artists' impressions, children's paintings, suitable clothing, and weather maps and forecasts.

Icy Icicles

Resources

- Images of icicles
- Paper and pencils
- Oil pastels and felt pens
- Paint and brushes
- Glitter
- Shiny paper

Approach

1 Begin by asking the children to draw spiky icicles all over the page, using a selection of oil pastels and felt pens. Encourage them to stick with a group of colours that could represent the cold. Blues, silver grey and dark purple can work well together.
2 Ask them to colour the images and to make spiky patterns on the page.
3 To finish the work, use small brushes to paint in between the oil pastels and pens.
4 Embellish the image with glitter and shiny paper.

A Winter Tree

Resources

- Images of trees in winter
- Paper
- Black felt pens
- Chalk

Approach

1 Look at images of trees in the winter. Discuss the shape of their branches and how they look so bare.
2 Use black felt pen to draw branches coming in from each side of the paper.
3 Ask the children to then use chalk around the branches to make an icy cold sky.

Weather and Words

An inspiring weather display can show contrast within the elements. Find an area in the room that is large enough to be split into sections to show the contrast between certain weather conditions.

Resources

- Paper and pencils
- Paint and brushes
- Collage materials (eg cotton wool, crêpe paper)
- Felt pens
- Card
- Scissors

Approach

1 Explain to the children that the display will be divided into four sections. Each will show an extreme weather condition, such as storms, gales/hurricanes, snow and heatwave.

2 Ask the children to paint each section using a variety of colours that will suit the chosen weather condition.

3 Encourage the children to think about texture when applying collage materials. Cotton wool, of course, works brilliantly as snow, and red crêpe paper adds warmth to the heatwave section. Ask them to source their own textures and materials which they think could be used to best illustrate the picture.

4 Invite the children to think of descriptive words that could accompany the display. They can design their own words using appropriate colours. These can be cut out of card or paper and added to the display.

Cross-curricular Links

- **Literacy/Drama** – Explore poetry that looks at the natural world and the weather, or has certain lines which mention weather conditions. 'I wandered lonely as a cloud', the first words of Wordsworth's 'Daffodils', make a great starting point. Ask the children to develop their own poems.

Religion and Citizenship

While teaching religious education we invite children to look at many different faiths and what they mean to individuals. Exploring artefacts can be an interesting visual way of making links with many different religions. Gather information and images of different religious artefacts from a variety of faiths and ask the children to read about and make drawings of these. Display their drawings side by side so they see many different religions together and become aware that each is as important as the other.

Sacred Texts

Resources

- Religious symbols (printed from the computer)
- Paper and pencils
- Red, brown, yellow and white card
- Scissors
- Red, brown, yellow and white oil pastels
- Coloured pens
- Gold and silver pens
- Ribbon
- Glue
- Shiny gold, red and orange paper

Approach

1 The children should research different sacred books before they start to design their own. Discuss the importance of religious books to different faiths. If possible the children should be given the chance to examine the books, looking at the text and layout. Encourage them to think about colour, pattern and shape.

2 Ask the children to cover a sheet of paper with different religious symbols. This can be photocopied and coloured in. When cut into strips it will be used as a border to the display.

3 Encourage the children to cut the book shapes from card. They will need to fold the books to create a spine.

4 Using oil pastels and pens, the children can add patterns and words. They can embellish these using the gold and silver pens.

5 Ask the children to decorate both sides of their book including the spine. They can even attach bits of ribbon and shapes cut out of shiny paper.

6 Arrange the children's designs onto the display board. All three sides of the book should be showing.

The Menorah

One of the oldest symbols in the Jewish faith is called the 'menorah'. It is a candelabrum with seven branches that is traditionally lit every evening and cleaned out every morning. The purest olive oil is used to light its lamps. The seven branches represent the branches of human knowledge and the Creation in seven days. The menorah used at Hanukkah has nine branches – eight for each of the days of Hanukkah and one lighting candle.

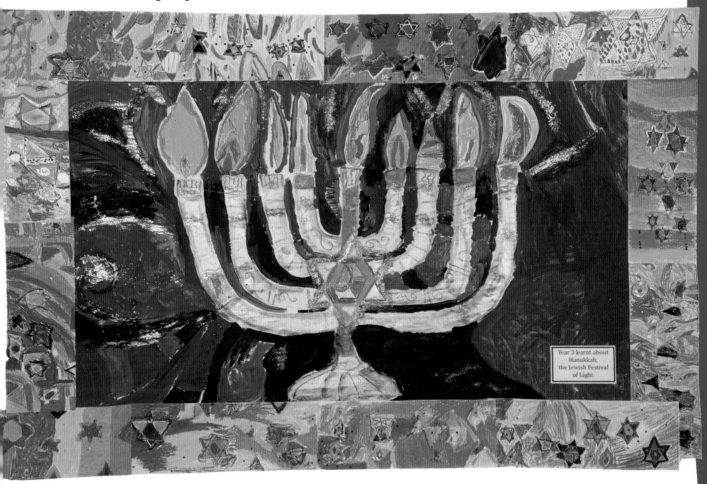

Year 3 learnt about Hanukkah, the Jewish Festival of Light.

Resources

- Images of a menorah
- Large piece of paper
- Paper and pencils
- Paint and brushes

Approach

1 Draw out and paint an image of a menorah. Encourage the children to fill the paper.
2 Ask the children to use black, navy and purple to paint the background. This will allow the menorah to stand out against the dark colours.
3 Use bright colours to paint the menorah and the flames.

Star of David

Resources

- Images of the Star of David
- Paper and pencils
- Oil pastels

Approach

1 Show the children images of the Star of David and discuss its significance.
2 Invite the children to draw images of the Star of David to form a pattern all over the paper.
3 Use oil pastels making sure the whole of the paper is filled with bright colours.
4 Display the images side by side, or use to frame the menorah display.

The Journey of Life

Encourage the children to reflect on and talk about the past. Discuss what memories are important to them and what past experiences have led to where they are now.

Road of Life Design

Resources

- Paper and pencils
- Card
- Felt pens
- Black paper/card
- White paint
- Green card
- Scissors
- Shiny gold paper
- Computer and printer

Approach

1 Encourage the children to think about key moments that occur throughout life and write down words connected with these.

2 Ask the children to draw road sign shapes on card. They can write their words inside these signs and decorate them.

3 Encourage the children to use black paper or card to make roads. White paint can be added to create lines.

4 The children can cut long grass out of different shades of green card, which will embellish the display.

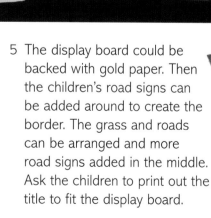

5 The display board could be backed with gold paper. Then the children's road signs can be added around to create the border. The grass and roads can be arranged and more road signs added in the middle. Ask the children to print out the title to fit the display board.

The Day of the Dead Display

El Día de los Muertos, the Day of the Dead, is a traditional Mexican holiday honouring the deceased. It is not an unhappy occasion, but rather a time of remembering and rejoicing. Families make an altar on which they place pictures of the deceased along with flowers and special items to remember loved ones by. Special candles are lit to burn throughout the night.

Resources

- Images of Day of the Dead artwork
- Paper and pencils
- Paint and brushes
- Felt pens
- Card
- Scissors

Approach

1 Invite the children to look at artwork inspired by the festival. Ask them to design and paint skulls using bright colours. They should think about flowers, stars, patterns and shapes to add detail to their drawings using felt pens.

2 Ask the children to paint sheets of flowers and patterns on paper or card. These can be cut into wide strips to make an interesting border to the display.

Cross-curricular Links

- **Geography/History** – Look at journeys made by individuals in the past. Investigate what strengths and skills were required for them to reach their destinations and achieve their goals.

67

Religious Buildings

Research and collect information about different religious buildings. Discuss with the children what these buildings mean to them. Encourage them to write about and discuss any experience they have of visiting or passing by a religious building. Collect images and make notes to form a small display about these buildings.

Religious Buildings Display

Resources

- Mixed card
- Scissors
- Oil pastels
- Felt pens
- Religious symbols (printed from the computer)
- Glue
- Shiny paper

Approach

1 Each table can work on creating a different type of religious building. The children should think about suitable symbols and the unique features of each building.

2 The children can cut the shape of their building out of card. They can begin to decorate these using oil pastels or felt pens. Encourage the children to print out any symbols and patterns that their building might feature. These can be cut out and glued onto their designs.

3 Arrange the religious buildings on the display board to resemble a town. Each one should be behind the other to conjure a sense of depth to the display.

4 Use shiny paper as a border to finish off.

Making a Mosque Together

This works very well as a group activity. Encourage the children to research images and to investigate mosques from around the world. Look closely at Islamic patterns and discover the colours often used within these. Encourage the children to try to design their own Islamic patterns. There are printable resources available from large bookshops or online that children can cut out, colour and embellish.

Resources

- Images of mosques
- Card
- Paper and pencils
- Felt pens
- Photocopiable images of Islamic patterns
- Scissors
- Glue
- Paint and brushes
- Shiny paper

Approach

1 Ask the children to draw out large individual mosque buildings, paying particular attention to the shapes they see in the images provided.

2 Ask the children to consider the colours they are going to use. Each section of the giant building has to work together, so it is important for the colours to be consistent.

3 Encourage the children to colour and cut out their images of the photocopiable Islamic patterns, or to draw their own.

4 Stick the images to the buildings.

5 Draw patterns over the buildings and invite children to paint small squares on their building or use shiny paper to make collage squares in order to give a mosaic effect.

6 Display their finished pieces together to form a huge mosque.

Looking to the Future

Ask the children to think about what their future holds. Discussing what they can do to make the right choices can make an inspirational starting point for a piece of artwork to uplift the classroom environment. This activity will encourage confidence and individuality. Discuss with them what skills and attributes they will need to work on to make a step towards the goals they want to achieve in their lives. Explain how being responsible, developing the necessary skills and considering what they want to achieve will help them in the right direction towards a positive and happy future.

Destiny Display

Resources

- Paper and pencils
- Card
- Felt pens
- Oil pastels
- Scissors
- Shiny paper
- Glue

Approach

1 Ask the children to think about what they want to achieve, and to draw and colour words to describe this.

2 Encourage them to make arrows out of card to represent a step in the right direction, and to decorate these with positive words that illustrate what they think they would like to achieve in their future.

3 Encourage the children to cut out colourful squares from shiny paper and to stick them side by side to form the background for the display.

4 Ask the children to draw and decorate doors to symbolise the future and what it holds.

5 Invite the children to cut out their words and to display them over the colourful background with the arrows and the doors.

Fitting Together

Resources

- Paper and pencils
- Paint and brushes
- Felt pens

Approach

1 Talk about how we all have to fit together and respect each other in the classroom to achieve a positive learning environment. Discuss how life is more harmonious if people try to work together, even though they may have different thoughts and beliefs.
2 Draw out puzzle pieces that fit together.
3 Use different colours to paint the pieces.
4 When dry, draw on figures and show them working and playing together.

Doors of Opportunity

Resources

- Coloured card
- Plain card
- Paper and pencils
- Felt pens
- Glue/stapler
- Scissors

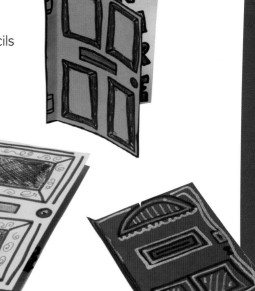

Approach

1 Ask the children to design and make a door using coloured card and to attach it on the left side, using glue or staples, to a piece of plain card.
2 Discuss with the children what they would like for their future and what actions they may need to take in order to achieve what they want.
3 In the space behind the door the children can draw and write about their hopes and ambitions for their future.
4 Display the doors so that they can be opened and read. Encourage the children and visitors to the classroom to open the doors of opportunity and read what is written behind each one.

Cross-curricular Links

- **Literacy** – Hold a sharing lesson, where each member of the class talks about themselves. Encourage pupils to listen to each other and to think about the lives of others in different cultures and societies.
- **Maths** – Investigate patterns. Look at repetition and tessellation. Ask children to devise and colour their own patterns that link and fit together.

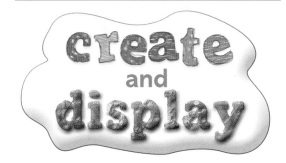

Titles in this series:

ISBN: 978-1-407-11915-1

SBN: 978-1-407-11918-2

ISBN: 978-1-407-11916-8

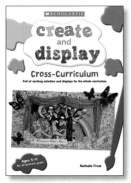

ISBN: 978-1-407-11917-5

ISBN: 978-1-407-12527-5 (Book)
ISBN: 978-1-407-12533-6 (CD-ROM)

ISBN: 978-1-407-12526-8 (Book)
ISBN: 978-407-12532-9 (CD-ROM)

ISBN: 978-407-12525-1 (Book)
ISBN: 978-407-12531-2 (CD-ROM)

ISBN: 978-407-12528-2 (Book)
ISBN: 978-407-12534-3 (CD-ROM)

ISBN: 978-1-407-12530-5 (Book)
ISBN: 978-407-12536-7 (CD-ROM)

ISBN: 978-1-407-12529-9 (Book)
ISBN: 978-407-12535-0 (CD-ROM)

To find out more, call: **0845 603 9091**
or visit our website **www.scholastic.co.uk**